Bernard of Clairvaux

The Honey-tongued Doctor

by
J.B. Midgley

*All booklets are published thanks to the
generous support of the members of the
Catholic Truth Society*

CATHOLIC TRUTH SOCIETY
PUBLISHERS TO THE HOLY SEE

Contents

The Honey-tongued Doctor 3

The Early Years 5

Citeaux: a Life of Asceticism 7

Clairvaux Monastery 13

Bernard's wider mission 17

Schism and its Aftermath 21

Eugenius III and the Second Crusade 27

The Good and Faithful Servant 33

The Writings of Saint Bernard 35

Devotion to Saint Bernard 50

Epilogue 53

The Honey-tongued Doctor

August 20th 1953 was the eight hundredth anniversary of the death of Saint Bernard of Clairvaux. Pope Pius XII chose this as the day on which to present his encyclical 'Doctor Mellifluous', the Honey-tongued Doctor and "last of those Fathers of the Church" who ensured its continued Apostolic mission that was entrusted by Christ.

In October 2009, Pope Benedict XVI reminded a Vatican Assembly of the importance and continued relevance of the monumental contribution Saint Bernard has made to the life of God's Church:

"Saint Bernard's writings remind us that questions about God and the meaning of life cannot be answered without prayer and contemplation. He who led the influential Cistercian monastery of Clairvaux for thirty-eight years put the love of God and Jesus Christ at the centre of his writings. His example is important because we sometimes try to resolve fundamental questions about God and man with reason alone. He shows us that without deep faith in God that is strengthened by prayer, contemplation and an intimate relationship with Our Lord, our reflections on the divine mysteries risk being mere intellectual excursions that lose credibility. It is right that he should be honoured as a talented administrator but, perhaps more significantly, he is renowned for his deep spirituality and love for Jesus and Mary."

Echoing his predecessor, Pope Benedict concluded, "as a Doctor of the Church, Saint Bernard has been regarded as 'the last of the Fathers', and his praises for Jesus so 'flowed like honey' that he is called 'Doctor Mellifluous', the Honey-tongued Doctor."

The Early Years

Tescelin Sorrel, an admired crusader and Lord of Fontaines near Dijon in Burgundy, was married to Aleth who was the daughter of the Lord of Montbard. Their union was blessed with six sons and one daughter, all of whom they dedicated to God when they were born, and it is a measure of their enlightened parentage that five of the children were raised to the honours of the altar as Saints or Blessed.

Birth and parentage

Bernard, the third son was born at Fontaines Castle in 1091. A local man, revered for the sanctity of his life, had foretold that the new arrival was destined to achieve great things and, accordingly, his parents made sure he would have the best possible preparation. When he was nine they enrolled him in the distinguished school of Chatillons-sur-Seine that was conducted by the Canons of Saint-Vorles.

Bernard soon impressed his teachers as an obedient, popular and talented boy. He showed a penchant for poetry and a wide range of literature that he valued as background preparation for the study of Holy Scripture and theology that would become like a second language to him. Centuries later, the eminent Catholic apologist

Bishop Jacques Bossuet would write, "Piety was his all, and most noticeable was his profound devotion to the Most Blessed Virgin Mary, and no one has spoken of the Queen of Heaven with more inspiration," though this holiness did not exclude a sense of fun and a ready turn of wit.

In 1110, Tescelin and the family suffered the loss of wife and mother Aleth who died on the feast of Saint Ambrose for whom she had always had a great devotion. Though he was only nineteen, Bernard now helped administer the estates especially when his father was away attending to business or fulfilling military commitments. He won universal respect and affection by his charitable consideration and efficiency. However he sorely missed his mother who had been a guiding light, helping him deal sensibly with the inevitable temptations and distractions of youth, and he began to think of withdrawing from the world to serve God in prayer and solitude.

Citeaux: a Life of Asceticism

Saint Robert of Molesme

Robert, (1027-1110), who was from a noble family in Champagne, joined the Benedictines and, in the course of time, became Prior of Moutier-la-Celle Abbey, later Abbot of Tonnerre, and then of the Hermits in the forest of Colan, a group that included the future founders of Citeaux, and Saint Bruno of Cologne who had abandoned a distinguished career and was destined to found the Carthusians.

Obedience to Saint Benedict's Rule

The Colan hermitage demonstrates that the vocation of an individual hermit was not necessarily permanent because, when his fame attracted others, they tended to adopt the monastic Rule to give cohesion to the community. The Hermits of Colan went to Molesme about 1075 with Robert as Abbot to lead them in exact obedience to Saint Benedict's Rule.

Unfortunately their reforming intentions were to be disappointed by the Abbey's acquisition of wealth with its consequent mitigation of austerity, the introduction of feudal practices, the entry of unsuitable novices, and the adoption of cultural, devotional and liturgical practices merely to accommodate the mood of the time.

In 1098, a group of some twenty monks led by Saint Alberic who was a former Colan hermit, and the English Saint Stephen Harding, asked Robert to undertake another reform and regenerate the observance of the Rule. The Lord of Beaune gave then some land at Citeaux, twelve miles from Dijon in the diocese of Chalon, described as "a place of horror, a vast wilderness, almost inaccessible by reason of thickets and thorns, and inhabited only by wild beasts."

It was in this rather uninviting place that the Archbishop of Lyons granted permission for a monastery to be opened with Robert as Abbot, Alberic as Prior and Stephen as sub-Prior. The Cistercian founders had chosen seclusion to worship God in prayer away from the bustle of the world, and to practice poverty in union with the poor Christ and all his impoverished people.

Like the early Christians, they would hold all things in common, sharing everything according to the needs of each member of a community that was united in mind and heart. Their clothing, diet and bedding would be basic and they would pay special attention to Chapter 73 of the Rule that admits it is "only the beginning of perfection, looking to the Desert Fathers who summon us along the true way to reach the Creator."

In Robert's absence, circumstances and observance at Molesme further deteriorated and monks who were well-disposed petitioned the Holy See for his return. Blessed Pope Urban II so instructed and Robert returned to rule as Abbot until his death in 1110. Alberic was then elected Abbot of Citeaux and remained so until his death nine years later. When Stephen succeeded him about 1112, he wrote a tender tribute to his predecessor: "He was a father, a friend, a fellow soldier, and a principal warrior in the Lord's battles who carried us all in his heart with affectionate love."

The Charter of Charity

Stephen Harding came from the West Country, probably Porlock in Somerset. He was a pupil at Sherborne Abbey before studying the liberal arts in Scotland and France but, after a visit to Rome, he decided to enter the religious life and joined the Benedictines of Molesme. He wrote the '*Carta Caritatis*', the wise and far-seeing Charter of Charity that embodied the early Cistercian constitution, guided the government of other monastic congregations, and established Citeaux's permanent and exalted position in the life of the Church.

The Charter's provisions included an annual visit by the Abbot of a founding house to affiliated houses, and the yearly attendance by all Superiors at a General Chapter at Citeaux. It safeguarded the original Cistercian spirit and observance by refraining from liturgical luxury, personal possessions, and declining to receive income from any dependent churches, property or accept customary offerings to the clergy.

The remote sites selected for foundations motivated the development of self-sufficiency techniques, and the welcome extended to lay-brothers whose vocation included farming the monastery's land, thus admitting to the religious life a wider section of the population than had previously been the case.

The lay-brothers' contribution and expertise allowed the choir-monks to devote themselves to public and private prayer, the meditative reading of sacred and spiritual reading, the '*Lectio Divina*', and their own manual labour as the Rule required. The celebration of Mass and the Divine Office by the "White Monks", with their undyed woolen habits, took less time than the more elaborate contemporary Benedictine liturgy but was, nevertheless, remarkable for its reverent and simple beauty.

Although scholarship did not feature as an original ambition in Cistercian life, Stephen's own appreciation of sculpture, books, manuscripts, and art encouraged the production of a new edition of the Bible in 1109. Despite the demands of the ascetic life and tilling the soil for sustenance, many scholars, theologians and spiritual writers emerged and Citeaux became a centre of monastic culture.

In addition, the community introduced liturgical reform, and classified authentic hymns and the melodies of Gregorian chant. Stephen's love of prayer and solitude did not impede his always being cheerful, welcoming, and universally loved. His charity was boundless and he opened the monastery's sparse coffers to all who were in any need, especially during a famine when even some of the community died.

To describe the early years of Citeaux as harsh would be an understatement but Providence was kind in the person of a noble lady, Elizabeth de Vergy, who gave farmland, vineyards and meadows to the hard-pressed community. Further relief arrived with an increase in vocations. The community received these blessings gratefully but did not waver in their determination to seek renewal, and preserve their separation from the world in simple poverty.

Bernard joins Citeaux

Bernard shared his thoughts about joining the religious life with family and friends, some of whom thought he had taken leave of his senses, especially when he mentioned Citeaux, but his personal powers of leadership were soon evident. In 1112, as Easter approached, he sought admission to the Citeaux novitiate with thirty other relatives and young nobles that included his brothers Bartholomew and Andrew, his cousin Robert of Chatillon, his uncle Gaudry who was famed as a soldier, and Hugh, Lord of Macon who would one day become Bishop of Auxerre. Since there had been no new novices at Citeaux for several years Abbot Stephen's welcome was all the warmer, and when their novitiate was successfully concluded, all but one professed to him their monastic vows of religion.

At first Bernard was allocated some lighter manual labour because he had some problems using a scythe but, with typical resolution, he persevered to conquer the implement! Thereafter, the number of those answering God's call to the religious life increased so rapidly that accommodation became insufficient. In 1113, therefore, Stephen opened the monasteries of La Ferte near Chalons, Pontigni in the Auxerre region, and another opportunity arose when Hugh Earl of Troyes gave some land on his estates.

Clairvaux Monastery

Stephen had quickly come to appreciate Bernard's remarkable progress in the religious life and his dedicated ability to undertake anything that would serve God's honour with efficiency. In 1115, he asked him to take a group of monks that included his two brothers to open a new house at Vallée d'Absinthe, the unpromising "Valley of Bitterness" in the Champagne diocese of Langres.

Transforming the Valley of Bitterness

That same year on June 25th, Bernard rechristened the place with the more hopeful 'Claire Vallée' or Clairvaux. In the absence of the Bishop of Langres, he was installed as abbot by William of Champeaux, the Bishop of Chalons-sur-Marne who was the distinguished Professor of Theology at Notre Dame and founder of the monastery of Saint Victor. He had already done all he could to help Bernard and his pioneer monks, and it was the beginning of a close and productive friendship.

The rigours of these first months can be imagined. The monks constructed simple cells for their initial accommodation, their meager diet consisted of coarse bread with herbs and beech leaves as vegetables, and the regime was punishing. This, and his personal austerities, took such toll on Abbot Bernard's health that William, supported by the General Chapter, ordered him to rest and personally supervised his convalescence.

Progress continued and soon one hundred and thirty new aspirants had come to place themselves under Bernard's direction. The latest arrivals included the rest of his brothers whom he clothed in the Cistercian habit, and then they were joined by his aged father Tescelin who ended his days and died peacefully as a monk of Clairvaux. Only his sister Humberline was left but, in 1124 with her husband's consent, she too entered the Cistercian convent of Jully that Stephen has opened some years earlier, and her name is commemorated among the saints.

God gives the increase

By 1118, the Clairvaux monastery was too small to house the increased number of monks, so Bernard commissioned groups to go and open the new foundations of Three Fountains, Fontenay and Foigny. The following year he attended the General Chapter convened by Stephen Harding and, though still only thirty, he commanded great attention and respect when he called upon all monastic orders to revive the early spirit of fervour and regularity. The Chapter articulated its adherence to the Cistercian constitution and to the directives of the 'Charter of Charity' which Pope Calixtus II confirmed on December 23rd 1119.

Magnetism and miracles

Shortly afterwards, Bernard's first recorded miracle took place when he restored speech to a relative who had been struck dumb and was able to make a good Confession of his many misdeeds before dying a few days later. He cured other sick people with the Sign of the Cross and, ever practical, did not recoil from giving relief to the fly-infested church in Foigny by excommunicating the visitors! This accounts for the old French reference to "the curse of the flies of Foigny".

In 1122, Bernard was invited to Paris to address the seminarians, and many were so moved by what he said and his magnetism that they returned with him to enter Clairvaux, perhaps to the chagrin of some Diocean Ordinaries! Similarly, when some German knights paid a visit on their travels and met the Abbot, they decided to stay, a conversion all the more remarkable since their previous interests were war and tournaments.

Others joined from less austere orders, their hearts touched by his charity, eloquence and humility. Centuries later, Erasmus the great humanist and friend of Saint Thomas More would say of him, "Bernard is an eloquent preacher more by nature than by art; he is full of charm and vivacity, and knows how to reach and move the affections."

Cluny

The Abbey of Cluny at Macon south of Dijon, founded in 909 by William the Pious, Duke of Aquitaine, became the centre of monastic development in the tenth and eleventh centuries, and was famed for its devotion to communal prayer, the elaboration of the Liturgy, and the choral office.

However, increased wealth and the relegation of manual labour's importance had somewhat distracted the monks from the Rule's primitive observance, and now they were not best pleased at the pre-eminence Citeaux was achieving among religious orders for fervent observance of the Rule. Bernard's wise and charitable intervention and the friendship he forged with Abbot Peter the Venerable of Cluny not only restored harmony but even inspired reform, though some monks of Cluny still chose to join Clairvaux.

Bernard's wider mission

Pope Calixtus II died on December 14th 1124, and a week later Cardinal Teobaldi was elected as Celestine II who was regarded as something of an anti-pope. Roman militia invaded the Conclave and forced him to resign in favour of Honorius II who, like Calixtus, was a reformer but more open to compromise than the 'Gregorians' who were devoted to the fundamental and essential reforms introduced by Pope Saint Gregory VII. A former monk of Cluny and one of the greatest Popes in history, his pontificate from 1073 to 1085 marked the turning point between the first Christian millennium and the second. In an effort to liberate the Church and the Papacy from secular control, he claimed temporal as well as spiritual authority over Christendom as well as opposing simony, clerical marriage and lay investiture, and insisted that metropolitan archbishops come to Rome to receive the pallium.

Knights Templar

In 1128, Pope Honorius convened the Council of Troyes under the presidency of Cardinal Matthew, the Bishop of Albano. Its purpose was to settle disputes that had arisen among the Paris bishops, and co-ordinate French ecclesiastical procedures. The attending prelates elected Bernard as Council Secretary and gave him the responsibility of publishing resultant decisions.

While at Troyes, he developed the Rule of the Knights Templar, a monastic, military order recently founded that soon became the ideal of French nobility. For more than a century, these Monk-knights fought bravely in the Crusades, undertook building programs, cared for the sick, and offered a protective presence for pilgrims to the Holy Land. They were later the subject of Bernard's eulogy, 'In Praise of a New Army', in which he encouraged them to conduct themselves with courage in their various endeavours.

Bernard did not hesitate to voice disapproval of unsuitable appointments to the episcopacy and other Church offices. Cardinal Harmeric wrote a letter from Rome rebuking him. "It is not fitting that noisy and troublesome frogs should come out of their marshes to trouble the Holy See and the Cardinals."

Undeterred, Bernard replied,

"If I have assisted at the Council, it is because I have been dragged to it as if by force. Now, illustrious Harmeric, if you so wished, who would have been more capable of freeing me from the necessity of assisting at the Council than yourself? Forbid these noisy frogs to leave their marshes, then your friend will no longer be exposed to accusations of pride and presumption."

He was unflinching in his belief that "a monk is as much a soldier of Christ as any other Christian, and has a duty to defend God's sanctuary." In this vein he wrote to the Dean of Languedoc,

"You may imagine that what belongs to the Church belongs to you while you officiate there. But you are mistaken, for though it is reasonable that one who serves the altar should live by the altar, yet it must not be to promote either his luxury of his pride."

Remarkable conversions

His plain speaking inspired some remarkable conversions including those of Archbishop Henry of Sens and Bishop Stephen of Paris both of whom renounced a rather worldly life that had involved spending most of their time at Court, and Abbot Suger of Saint-Denis who relinquished a brilliant political career as chief adviser to King Louis VII to return to the monastic life.

Increasingly, Bernard won golden opinions, so much so that it was said he had been sent to govern the Western Church from his isolated monastery. If so, it was at great cost to himself, and his rueful reflection may comfort those who sometimes feel that dealing with the affairs of the world and supporting others make too many intrusions on their religious life and aspirations.

"Life is overrun everywhere by anxieties, suspicions and cares. There is scarcely an hour free from the crowd of discordant appellants and the troubles and cares of their business. I have no power to stop them coming and cannot refuse to see them, and they do not leave me time even to pray."

Universally revered

Bernard had become universally revered for his learning, wisdom, sanctity and gifts as a mediator. He was called upon by princes to settle disputes, bishops to solve diocesan problems, popes for his advice, bishops to solve diocesan problems, as well as appeals from individual clergy and laity. It was obvious that he was one of those whose gifts and opportunities were exactly matched, and who possessed a far-reaching and irresistible spiritual magnetism.

His influence extended far beyond Clairvaux as he defended the rights of the Church against secular rulers who were trying to appropriate ecclesiastical authority including that of appointing prelates, and corrected French bishops who were showing ill-judged submission to kings and princes. According to the Chroniclers, this period saw a succession of miracles through Bernard's prayers that brought relief to the sick and distressed.

Schism and its Aftermath

When Pope Honorius died in 1130, two Popes were elected! The moderate reformers chose Innocent II, while ultra-conservatives voted for Peter Leonitus, an ambitious former monk of Cluny who took the name Anacletus II. Having managed to attain political influence in Rome, his first act was to banish Innocent who was forced to take refuge in Pisa.

A man of great influence

A council of French bishops assembled at Etampes and invited Bernard to choose between the rival Pontiffs. He selected Innocent with the support of his friends Saint Hugh, Bishop of Grenoble, and Saint Norbert, Archbishop of Madgeburg and founder of the Order of the Canons regular of Premontre. The decision was accepted by the great Catholic powers that included King Louis "the Large" of France who received the Pope with appropriate honour. At Chartres, Bernard also persuaded Henry I of England to acknowledge the validity of Innocent's election, and secured the support of Count William of Poitiers who had previously favoured Anacletus. That accomplished, and all the while reconciling competing factions, he escorted Innocent back to Italy and then on to Germany to meet Emperor Lothaire II who offered to support Bernard's choice if he were given the right to appoint bishops. Bernard corrected him so comprehensively that he withdrew the condition and co-operated in preparing to be crowned by Innocent in Rome.

However, the problem was not entirely solved. In May 1132, when Innocent and Lothaire entered Rome, they were unable to cope with the hostile adherents of Anacletus and had no option but to leave, the one to Pisa and the other "to beyond the Alps." Bernard returned to France to continue the work of reconciliation that involved bringing schismatic lords and troublesome prelates to a better frame of mind. He then hurried back to Italy to make sure Roger of Sicily did not coerce the citizens of Pisa to withdraw loyalty to Innocent.

Next he brought the city of Milan back to obedience to the Pope and was so revered there as "a man sent from Heaven, a saintly scholar and a worker of miracles", that he was invited to be Archbishop. His humility led him to decline as it would when he was later offered the Sees of Genoa, Reims, Langres and Chalons. Had he so wished there would have been no limits to his advancement. These brief references to his travels around Europe at that time hardly reveal the physical demands, dangers and self-sacrifice involved.

In that same year of 1132, Bernard sent monks under the leadership of his secretary William, later venerated as a saint, to found Rievaulx Abbey after discussion with King Henry I of England and Baron Walter Espec who donated the land. The Abbeys of Tintern and Fountains were to follow and all three, even in ruins, still inspire wonder at what these monks achieved in honouring God. Other Cistercian Abbeys that were to grace England and Wales, and recognised by David Farmer in his '*Benedict's Disciples*', include Ryland, Roche, Bordsley, Cwmhir, Cymmer, Whitland, Neath, Margam, Hailes, Woburn, Rewley, Stanley, Waverley, Netley, Beaulieu, and the first Buckfast.

'Song of Songs': Jesus as friend and lover

It must have been with some relief that back in the peace of the cloister, Bernard was able to resume his writing, particularly the eighty-six homilies on the 'Song of Songs' that Hebrew tradition had attributed to Solomon. Origen, the third century Biblical commentator and theologian, was a man of prayer whose spiritual life was supported by scholarship, and his commentary on the 'Song of Songs' inspired lasting interest in this anthology of love poems as an allegory of God's relationship with the Church and each of His children. Bernard's homilies awakened Christian devotion to the human Jesus as friend and lover who "like a mother hen gathers her chickens beneath her protective wings, a tender Mother who loves, feeds and instructs." In this respect, his own thinking and spiritual experience brought new meaning to the text.

Diplomacy and growth

In 1137, Pope Innocent interrupted Bernard's solitude by asking him to settle a quarrel that had arisen between Lothaire and Robert of Sicily and was adversely affecting the Church. Not only did he succeed but he even convinced Roger and Peter of Pisa of Innocent's right to the Papal throne.

Anacletus died in 1138 and with him the Schism. In the meantime, it was wonderful that men were coming from all over Europe to Clairvaux, but there were problems of overcrowding. Bernard responded by sending monks to establish daughter foundations throughout the Continent with marked success in Germany, Sweden, Ireland, Portugal, Switzerland and Italy, in addition to those already flowering in England and Wales. At Innocent's request, Clairvaux monks also assumed administration of the Abbey of Saints Vincent and Anastasius in Rome.

In 1139, Innocent called the Second Lateran Council finally to heal the wounds the recent schism had inflicted on the Church, ratify his claim to the Papacy, and discipline all who had been involved in the schism. Bernard was in attendance of course, and the Pope acted upon his recommendation to forgive the transgressions. The Council then reaffirmed the reforms that Pope Saint Gregory VII had introduced, and added its own disciplinary canons to reflect the needs of the changing world of the twelfth century. Bernard was inevitably called upon to quell residual disturbances affecting the Church, tasks he accomplished with characteristic diplomacy and charity.

Saint Malachy

Shortly after the Lateran Council, Bernard was visited at Clairvaux by Saint Malachy, 1094-1148, who was then Archbishop of Armagh, Metropolitan and Primate of the Church in Ireland, a distinguished pioneer of Gregorian reform, and a protector of the monastic Rule. A close friendship immediately developed between the two champions of the Faith that, among other activities, led to the Cistercian foundation in 1142 of Mellifont Abbey that, in turn became the mother-house of many affiliated monasteries.

Malachy dearly wished to take the Cistercian habit himself and join Clairvaux, but this required papal permission which Pope Innocent declined to grant. In 1148 on his way to Rome on behalf of the Irish Church he called at Clairvaux, where he fell mortally ill, and died peacefully in the arms of his friend Bernard.

Peter Abelard

The closing years of the eleventh century had witnessed the emergence of a strong spirit of independent thinking in politics and religion that was not entirely removed from the personal ambition of some major proponents. Foremost among the advocates who exalted the free exercise of human reason and logic was the French theologian Peter Abelard, (1079-1142), whose insistence on the primacy of dialectic in theological reflection caused such concern that his views were rejected at the Council of Sens, (1140-1141).

Bernard's position was that the mere rationalisation of religious belief could be dangerously misleading, and he defended "faith not as an opinion but as a certitude." When Abelard asked to meet him in debate, he found it difficult to reply to Bernard's cogent presentation. He subsequently retired to the Abbey of Cluny where the saintly Peter the Venerable was still Abbot, and ended his days not long afterwards in tranquility.

Eugenius III and the Second Crusade

Pope Innocent II's death in 1143 was followed by two brief pontificates. That of Celestine II, an elderly scholar and reformist, lasted seven months. His successor Lucius II survived only a year, during which time he had to endure strong opposition from an independent and critical senate that had been established by the brother of the late anti-pope Anacletus.

First Cistercian Pope

On February 15th 1145, Bernard of Pisa, Abbot of the Roman Abbey of Saints Vincent and Anastasius and one of Bernard's spiritual sons, became the first Cistercian Pope who is now remembered as Blessed Eugenius III. During his eight year pontificate he wore his religious habit, lived according to the Rule, and was unswerving in his commitment to the fulfilment of monastic and clerical ideals.

A few months after the election of Eugenius, Cardinal Alberic who was the papal legate to France asked Bernard to come to Languedoc where an offshoot of the Albigensian heresy had emerged and was making dangerous progress. The erroneous philosophy was based on the "absolute dualism" of two battling eternal powers, the Good Spirit and the Evil-Matter. In this conflict, human salvation is in a process of alignment with the good God in which the soul is liberated from the contamination of the flesh, and the Good Spirit ultimately prevails over the inferior Evil-Matter. Though he was ill at the time, Bernard answered the call, preaching, working miracles, and restoring orthodoxy in Southern France.

Illuminating the papacy

Pope Eugenius asked Bernard to write a comprehensive treatise on papal spirituality. The resultant five books of considerations proposed that Church reform is initially dependent on the sanctity of the Pope, and continues by accepting that temporal concerns are secondary to a pious and meditative approach to discussion and consequent action.

Bernard distinguished between the authority of the Pope and that of papal civil servants, pointing out that the "the murmuring of the churches will not stop unless the Roman Curia cease to judge untried cases just as it pleased and without the accused being present."

He saw such distorted centralisation as disrespectful to the dignity of Papal authority and confusing for bishops, clergy and laity. Appeals merely to Curial offices did not serve justice and he reminded Eugenius that, "you are the successor of Peter, not of Constantine. Remember that Peter knew nothing of silks and gold, or riding a white horse escorted by soldiers, or surrounded by attendants acclaiming him aloud."

'*On Consideration*', with the illuminating passages on the Papacy, has been appreciated by many who have since occupied the Chair of Peter, including the convener of the Second Vatican Council Blessed Pope John XXIII, (1958-1963), who said it was his bed-time reading.

Second Crusade

The Crusades were a series of wars fought for the recovery or defense of Christian lands from Muslim occupation, and especially for the liberation of Jerusalem and the Holy Land. On Christmas Day 1144, the Seljuk Turks defeated the Christians at the siege of Edessa, and took this chief city of one of the principalities established by the First Crusade. In 1146, Pope Eugenius summoned the Second Crusade in response to appeals by the Armenian bishops and King Louis VII of France that steps be taken to recapture Edessa before Jerusalem, Antioch and other Crusader states suffered a similar fate.

The Pope asked Bernard to preach this "Holy War" to which he attached the same Indulgences that had been granted the First Crusade, mainly that those who carried the Crusade Cross merited the remission of the temporal punishment due to sin.

On Palm Sunday, March 31st, a parliament met in Burgundy at Vezelay, the location of the Benedictine

Abbey that was famous as the rumoured site of Saint Mary Magdalene's relics, and a popular shrine for visiting pilgrims. Bernard preached to an assembly so great that it gathered in a field, and spoke with "eloquent conviction and heartfelt persuasion in the presence of King Louis, Queen Eleanor and the nobility. Afterwards, so many princes and lords knelt before him that he had to use strips of his outer habit to make the traditional Crosses sufficient to satisfy the ardour of all who wished to join the Crusade."

Such great support also came from citizens that he wrote to the Pope, "Cities and castles are now empty. There is not left one man to seven women, and everywhere there are widows to still living husbands." To encourage the enterprise further, he went to Germany where his preaching and reported miracles brought an equally enthusiastic response that was led by the Emperor Conrad and his nephew Frederick Barbarossa to whom he presented the Crusader's Cross.

Faith as persuasion not coercion

At this time, an anti-Semite and unbalanced monk called Raoul was stirring up hatred of the Jewish people by accusing them of not contributing to the cost of protecting Jerusalem. Conscious that persecution of the Jews had escalated from the eleventh century, Bernard protested against such unjust treatment of these ancestors in the faith. He maintained that conversion is a matter of persuasion not coercion, and roundly berated and silenced Raoul in the language Saint John had used for the Devil: "I suppose it is enough for you to be as your master. He was a murderer from the beginning and the father of lies" (*cf. Jn 8:44; Sermon 356*).

Unjustly blamed

In 1147, when Pope Eugenius went to France to maintain momentum for the Crusade, he took the opportunity to call a council in Paris to dispel confusion caused by Gilbert, Bishop of Poitiers who was voicing the opinion that the essence and attributes of God are not God, that those of the Father, Son and Holy Spirit are not the Persons themselves, and that therefore the Divine Nature did not become incarnate. Naturally, it was Bernard he asked to articulate a profession of faith to correct the theories of Gilbert who accepted the decision in obedience. Eugenius then visited Clairvaux where he presided over the Cistercian General Chapter and saw at first hand the remarkable results of Bernard's leadership.

When the Second Crusade turned out to be a lamentable disaster, Bernard was unjustly blamed. The causes were more the misconduct and double dealing of some participants, the over-confidence, indiscipline and looting on the part of the German knights and foot-soldiers, the blunders of Christian nobles who failed at the siege of Damascus, the treacherous greed of others in Syria, and the intrigues of Queen Eleanor and the Prince of Antioch.

Although the criticism heaped upon him was wholly misdirected, Bernard's humility obliged him to write an apology to the Pope. This appears in the second part of '*On Consideration*' where he adds that "the Crusaders, like the Hebrew people, had been favoured by the Lord but, in both cases, misdeeds and infidelity have brought misfortune and misery."

The Good and Faithful Servant

In 1152, Bernard began to contemplate that his life was drawing to a close. He was approaching only his sixty-third year but, as a result of his ceaseless labours, travel and self-denial, his health had been delicate for most of his adult and working life. His thoughts became even more focused by the deaths of some of his contemporaries. These included Emperor Conrad, his son Henry, and Abbot Suger of whom he said, "If there is any precious vase adorning the palace of the King of Kings it is the soul of the venerable Suger."

The false accusations related to the Second Crusade's failure were an added sadness and he commented, "I have long dwelt in Heaven in desire, but this desire is weakness rather than piety. The saints were moved to pray for death out of a longing to see Christ, but I am driven hence by scandals and evil."

The death of Blessed Pope Eugenius III in July 1153 was also a devastating blow that deprived him of a treasured friend, consoler and supporter.

If that were not enough, the Archbishop of Trier asked him to come and settle a dispute between the Duke of Lorraine and the citizens of Metz whom he had subjugated. Although he was in no fit state, he responded with typical willingness and managed to persuade both sides to settle their difference without resorting to arms, and accept the treaty he drew up for them.

The situation he left was reasonably harmonious, but he returned to Clairvaux a dying man. On August 20th 1153, he received the Last Sacraments in the presence of many of his community that, despite their apostolate and the foundation of so many daughter houses, still numbered seven hundred.

He told them, "the barren tree should be rooted up and the unprofitable servant should not occupy a place uselessly." Then he peacefully yielded his soul to God whom he had served so valiantly with never a thought of self. Fittingly, his resting place was before Our Lady's altar in the Abbey Church.

During Bernard's thirty-eight years as Abbot, Clairvaux had become the spiritual centre of Europe and, at various times, his disciples included a Pope, an Archbishop of York, and a multitude of Cardinals and Bishops. His monks had established sixty-eight affiliated foundations that, in turn, grew to close on four hundred throughout the West.

The Writings of Saint Bernard

As these were the subject of the Holy Father's address, it seems appropriate to begin by offering some brief extracts that rekindle admiration for this supremely gifted spiritual writer who, for forty years, was the most influential voice in Christendom, and still continues to teach us from Heaven.

Though he loved prayerful solitude, Bernard took every opportunity to instruct by good example, with dedication and a natural eloquence adapted sensitively to his various audiences. His sermons, letters and treatises express the ideals of the founders of the Cistercian Order, articulate a theology of reformed monasticism for the benefit of his monks, and reveal a mystic who believed that contemplation leads to "the love in action" that is exemplified in the life of Jesus who brings us closer to God and fulfils His intention for us.

The quality of Bernard's teaching, the fervour with which he spoke, and the inspiration of his monastic theology led his own brethren and others, particularly the Carthusians, to ask that he commit everything in writing for the benefit of his contemporaries and posterity. He responded to their request and completed his first work, '*Steps in Humility and Pride*' in 1120.[1]

On Loving God

Written at the request of the Carthusians and his own community, this has been described as Bernard's masterpiece to which he added his *'Letter on Love'*. It reveals the importance with which Cistercians regarded the function of the will in recognising the relationship of divine and human love in the life of grace.

"I said that the reason for our loving God is God, and I spoke the truth because He is the prime mover of our love and final end. He Himself is the source of our human love, for He gives the power to love and brings desire to its consummation. He is lovable in His essential Being and gives Himself to be the object of our love, willing that our love for Him will bring us to happiness. His love opens the way to ours and is our love's reward. He leads us kindly in love's way and generously returns the love we give. How sweet He is to those who wait for Him, how rich to all who call upon Him, for He can give them nothing better than Himself.

Love is the only motion, sense and affection of the soul by which the creature, in his inadequate way, can reciprocate in kind. When God loves, He wishes to be loved only in return. Assuredly, He loves for no other reason than to be loved. He knows that those who love Him are happy in their love. Even though the creature by his nature loves less than the Creator, he lacks nothing if he loves with all his being. Such love is self-sufficient; it is pleasing to itself and its own reward." (*cf. Sermon 83 and the Office of Readings, the Divine Office for August 20th from 'On the Song of Songs'*).

The Most Blessed Virgin Mary

In his homilies '*In Praise of Mary*', Bernard inspired devotion to Our Lady whom he saw as the channel of all grace and the dispenser of love from Heaven. His prayer to Mary, the "*Memorare*" is, after the "Hail Mary", perhaps the most frequently used Marian Prayer by Christians of all denominations throughout the world.

"Remember O most loving Virgin Mary, that never was it known that anyone who fled to your protection, implored your help, or sought your intercession was left unaided. Inspired by this confidence, we fly unto you, O Virgin of virgins, our Mother! To you we come, before you we stand, sinful and sorrowful. O Mother of the Word Incarnate, despise not our petitions, but in your mercy hear and answer us. Amen".

His tender invocation 'O clement, O loving, O sweet Virgin Mary' was later added to the '*Salve Regina*', and his homilies in her praise inspired other saints like Alphonsus Ligouri, (1696-1787), when he wrote his '*Mariolgy, the Glories of Mary*' and described her as the "Gate to Heaven".

Bernard tells us, "in dangers, in doubts, think of Mary, call upon Mary. Do not let her name leave your lips nor your heart. So that you will more certainly obtain the assistance of her prayer, do not neglect to walk in her footsteps. With her as guide, you will never go astray; while calling to her you will never lose heart. As long as you think of her, you will never be deceived. While she holds your hand you cannot fall. Under her protection you have nothing to fear. If she walks before you, you shall not grow weary and you will reach your goal."

The famed mediaeval poet Dante Aligheri, (1265-1321), was twenty-five when his beloved friend Beatrice died. He credited her with being the inspiration of his life and work, especially the *'Divina Comedia'* in which she is his guide in the last Canto, 'Paradiso', that concludes with the celebration of "the love that moves the sun and the stars."

Dante was in awe at Bernard's contemplative mysticism, his devotion to Mary and his eloquence and thus chose him as the final poet of 'Paradiso'. The Saint prays to the Blessed Virgin that Dante's earthly love for Beatrice will bring him the grace to come to the vision of the all-loving God, and the supreme mysteries of the Trinity and Unity of God, and the Incarnation. He is entrusted with the poet's concept that Mary, the Virgin, conceived the Father and, by the power of the Holy Spirit, gave birth to Him as the Son in the Incarnation. His tribute to Our Lady was translated by Monsignor Ronald Knox as the Hymn, 'Maiden yet a Mother, Daughter of thy Son' (*cf. Westminster Hymnal 114*).

Saint John Baptist De La Salle

The eminent French theologian, educator and founder of the Brothers of the Christian Schools, Saint John Baptist De La Salle, (1652-1719) also held Bernard in profound reverence. He always observed his feast of August 20th in prayer and recollection, asking God to grant him a share in the Saint's fervent spirit and fidelity to the Rule.

He was inspired by Bernard's expressions of devotion to the Most Blessed Virgin when he wrote '*Meditations for the Feasts of Our Lady*' for his Brothers, particularly her Immaculate Conception, her Divine Maternity, and her Birthday on September 8th when she is honoured as the Mediatrix of all Graces.

"We should have a great devotion to the Most Blessed Virgin so greatly honoured by the Eternal Father who has placed her in rank above all others because she bore in her womb Him who is equal to Himself. She is raised above all other creatures by the abundance of grace she has received and by the unequalled purity of the life. God who does all things with wisdom, having decreed the salvation of men by the birth of a Redeemer like unto them, was pleased to choose a Virgin as His temple and habitation. To prepare her for such as He desired, He conferred upon her by the Holy Spirit all the natural and supernatural qualities befitting the Mother of God. If we love Jesus and are loved by Him, we must be loved by the Most Blessed Virgin. Just as there is a close relation between Jesus and His holy Mother, so all who love Jesus and are loved by Him, greatly honour Mary and are cherished by her."

The Holy Trinity

"Among all things called one, the unity of the Divine Trinity holds the first place. How can plurality consist with unity, or unity with plurality? To examine the fact closely is rashness, to believe it is piety, to know it is life, and life eternal.

The immaculate law of God is charity. It is called law either because He lives by it or because no one possesses it except by His gift. Nor is it absurd for me to say that God lives by law since law is nothing else than charity. Foe what preserves that supreme and ineffable unity in the supreme and Blessed Trinity but charity? Charity then is a law and it is the Law of the Lord that unites the Trinity in the bond of peace."

The Annunciation

"Mary, you have heard that you will conceive and bear a Son; you have heard that you will conceive, not of Man, but of the Holy Spirit. The Angel is waiting for your answer; it is time for him to return to God who sent him. We too are waiting O Lady. To you the price of our salvation is offered. If you consent, straightaway we shall be freed."

Advent and the Incarnation

"Our Lord's first coming is in the flesh and in weakness; another coming is hidden as souls see within themselves, receive rest and consolation, and are saved. His last coming will be in glory and majesty, and all flesh shall see the salvation of our God.

Behold, peace is no longer promised but conferred, no longer delayed but given, no longer predicted but bestowed. In the fullness of the Godhead, Jesus comes in the flesh to manifest Himself to our earthly minds, so that when His humanity appeared, His kindness might also be acknowledged. Where the humanity of God appears, His kindness can no longer be hidden."

Christmas

"Comfort is here; help has come from Heaven. 'The kindness and humanity of God our Saviour has appeared.' The kindness has always been there because the Lord's mercy is from everlasting though hidden until humanity appeared. Peace is no longer promised but sent, no longer prophesied but given to us. The Father has sent a sackful of mercy to earth, a sack that must be rent in the Passion so that the price of our Redemption may pour from it. Though a little sack, it is full. Indeed it is a Child who is given to us but in Him dwells the fullness of the Godhead for, when the fullness of time came, the fullness of the Godhead also arrived."

The Epiphany of the Lord

"He came in flesh to show Himself to all people living in flesh, and His humanity appeared so that all may know His kindness. How could He show His kindness to me better then by taking my flesh, that is my flesh not Adam's before the Fall. He showed His mercy by assuming our misery, and the smaller He made himself, the kinder He showed Himself. The smaller He is made for me, the dearer He is."

The Holy Family

"'He was subject to them.' God, to whom the angels are subject, was subject to Mary and Joseph without doubt. Learn O Man to obey, learn O Earth to submit. God humbles Himself, and yet do you exalt yourself? He becomes subject to men, and yet are you eager to lord it over others, place yourself above your Maker? If you cannot follow Him wherever He goes, at least follow in the way He has come down to you."

The Holy Name

"No voice can sing, no heart can frame, nor can the memory find a sweeter sound than Jesus name, the Saviour of Mankind. Christians invoke the Holy name of Jesus with absolute confidence in Him who saves and who said, 'If you ask the Father anything in my name, He will give it to you.' Seventy-two disciples came back from their mission rejoicing that the devils had submitted, and in all the wonders that had been accomplished in Jesus' name. His last words before ascending to His Father with our human nature, give a message that fills with confidence all who believe in His name: 'In my name they will cast out devils, they will have the gift of tongues, they will pick up snakes in their hands and, should they drink any deadly poison, they will be unharmed; they will lay their hands on the sick who will recover.'"

The Sacred Heart

"How good and pleasant a thing it is to dwell in the heart of Jesus! Who is there that does not love a heart so wounded? Who can refuse a return of love to a heart so loving?

Jesus, how sweet is the thought of you, giving true joy to the heart, surpassing honey and all sweetness in His own presence. Nothing more sweet can be proclaimed, nothing more pleasant can be heard, and nothing more loving can be thought of than Jesus, the Son of God.

Jesus, the hope of penitents, how kind you are to those who pray. How good to those who seek you - but what joy to those who find. No tongue can tell, nor can the written word express it: only one who knows from experience can say what it means to love Jesus. May you, O Jesus be our joy as you will be our reward. In you be our glory forever.

Jesus says, 'First learn to love yourself, then you can love me.' By His first work, He gave me to myself, by the next He gave Himself to me, and when He gave me Himself, He gave me back myself."

Passiontide

"I will remind myself of all the labours Jesus undertook in His preaching, His weary journeys, His temptations during His fast, His vigilance in prayer, His tears of compassion. I will also remember His sorrows, and the insults, spits, blows, mocking, rebukes, the nails, and all the sufferings that rained down on Him."

Bernard has been credited with the authorship of the verses that begin "Salve Caput Cruentatum" that have been variously translated, first by J.W.Alexander, and later by Monsignor Ronald Knox for the Westminster Hymnal as "O Sacred Head ill-used, by read and bramble scarred"... (*WH 41*).

The Sacrifice of the Mass

"With a single Mass heard with the necessary devotion, one procures more good than if he were to give all he possessed to the poor and make the longest pilgrimage."

The Good Shepherd

"He is the Good Shepherd who gives His life for His sheep, His life for them, His flesh to them: the one for Redemption, the other for their food. O mighty marvel. He is Himself the Shepherd of the sheep, their Pasture and their Redemption's price."

Call to Conversion

"If you desire to be satisfied and would like this desire to be fulfilled, start by being hungry for righteousness and you cannot fail to be satisfied. Yearn for the loaves in your Father's house and you will be disgusted with the husks of swine. Try, however little, to experience the taste of righteousness and then you will both desire and merit more. 'Those who eat me will hunger for more; those who drink me will thirst for more'" (*Sermons on Conversion;* cf. *Lk* 15:1ff; *Si* 24:21).

In the shelter of the Most High

Bernard was keenly aware of God's Providence that encompasses the Holy Spirits, and what Our Lord says about the immense spiritual world that features in our lives in the material world as we prepare to join the Angels. "I tell you, if anyone openly declares himself for me in the presence of men, the Son of Man will openly declare Himself for him in the presence of God's angels" (*Lk* 9:26). He accordingly encouraged the devotion to the Angels that early monasticism had initiated and developed, with the comfort that each one has a Guardian Angel who is with us at all times and in all places.

"'He has given His angels charge over you to keep you in all your ways'. You will see the angels of God ascending and descending upon the Son of Man. They ascend because of Him, and they descend, or rather condescend, because of us. The blessed spirits descend by contemplating God and, out of compassion, to 'keep you in all your ways.' They ascend to God's face and descend at His bidding, for 'He has given His angels charge over you.' Yet, in descending, they do not lose the vision of His glory because 'they always behold the Face of the Father.' They imitate the example of the Only-Begotten who came to serve His disciples. They act from love alone and you too descend and condescend as you show mercy to your neighbours and strive to ascend with eager soul to sublime and eternal truth, to Him who is truth and mercy itself." (*cf. 'Ascending and Descending', in Sermons on Conversion*).

Meditation on the 'Song of Songs'

"'I sought Him whom my soul loves.' Now is the acceptable time; now is the day of salvation. It is the time for seeking and calling because often His presence is sensed before He is called. Hear His promise, 'Before you call me, I will answer. See I am here.' The Psalmist also describes the Bridegroom's generosity. 'The Lord hears the crying of the poor; His ear hears the movement of their hearts.' If God is to be sought through good works, then let us do good to all while we have time, all the more because the Lord says the night is coming when no one can work. Will you find any other time in ages to come to seek God or do good, except the time when He has ordained that He will remember you? Today is the day of salvation because God our King before all ages has been working salvation in the midst of the earth."

Poverty, Chastity and Obedience

"Poverty was not found in Heaven. It abounded on earth, but human beings did not know its value. The Son of God treasured it, and came down from Heaven to choose it for Himself, and so make it precious to us. Theirs is an endless road, a hopeless maze, who seek for goods before they seek for God. Those attached to this world think we are playing about when we shun what they most like and pursue what they flee from. The game we play is joyful, praiseworthy and delights those who are watching from Heaven."

When John Baptist De La Salle spoke of 'the lovely and treasured virtue of Chastity', he referred to Bernard's observation that 'though the struggle to preserve it is a bloodless martyrdom it is nonetheless painful'. He followed Bernard in asking his Brothers to consider the very soul of true Obedience.

"The most powerful means and easiest way of becoming perfectly obedient is to recognise God in the person of the Superior, persuading oneself that it is Our Lord who commands by way of his mouth." He urged them to emulate Saint Bernard by asking themselves why they had come and if it were to command or obey."

Community Life

"If there should be a monastery without an awkward and ill-tempered member, it would be necessary to go and find one and pay him his weight in gold, so great is the profit that results from this trial when it is used properly.

If you are wise, you will show yourself rather as a reservoir than a canal. For a canal spreads abroad the water it receives but a reservoir waits until it is filled before overflowing, and thus shares its superabundance of water without loss to itself."

Manual Labour

"He who labours as he prays, lifts his heart to God with his hands. Arouse yourself, gird your loins, put idleness aside, grasp the nettle and do some hard work.

Idleness is the enemy of the soul. Therefore, the brothers should have specified periods for manual labour…When they live by the labour of their own hands, as did our fathers and the Apostles, then they are really monks" (*quoting Saint Benedict's Rule Ch 48*).

Self Appraisal

"If you notice something evil in yourself, correct it; if something good, take care of it; if something beautiful, cherish it; if something unhealthy, heal it. Do not weary of reading the Lord's commandments, and then you will know what to avoid and what to attain. When you are content with the testimony of you own conscience, you will not want to shine with the light of someone else's praise.

Whether in this life or in death or in the resurrection, the body is of great service to the soul that loves the Lord. First it produces the fruits of penitence, second, it brings the gift of rest, and third, the final state of beatitude.

All things are possible to one who believes. He alone is God who can never be sought in vain, even when He cannot be found."

Devotion to Saint Bernard

The sons and daughters of Saint Benedict honour Bernard because of the wonderful activity and expansion he generated, and the reforms he inspired. He was so regarded as a saint that the unofficial devotion of the faithful began even during his lifetime, and he was officially canonised by Pope Alexander III in 1174.

The feast of this, the first Cistercian Saint, was entered in the Church's universal calendar on August 20th, the anniversary his death. Pope Pius VIII declared him a Doctor of the Church in 1830 and, as mentioned earlier, Pope Pius XII hailed him as "Doctor Mellifluous", the Honey-tongued Doctor, in 1953. Understandably, he is the heavenly Patron of Beekeepers as well as candle makers, Gibraltar, Speyer Cathedral, and Queens College Cambridge.

Representations in Art

The Apparition of the Blessed Virgin Mary to Saint Bernard by Filippo Lippi that is in the Badia, Florence; 'Bernard exorcising possession', an altar piece by Jorg Breu; 'True effigy of Bernard of Clairvaux' by Georg Andreas Wasshuber; and his emblems in other portrayals are a pen, bees, and the instruments of the Passion.

From the Liturgy

"O blessed Bernard whose soul was enlightened with the wonders of the eternal Word; he spread the light of faith and true teaching throughout the Church (*Benedictus Antiphon, Morning Prayer*).

Lord God, you made Saint Bernard burn with zeal for your house, and gave him grace to enkindle and enlighten others in your Church. Grant that by his prayer we may be filled with the same spirit, and always live as children of the light (*Morning Prayer*).

Bernard, Doctor of the Church, from whom teaching flowed like sweet honey, friend of the Divine Bridegroom and herald telling of the wonders of the Virgin Mother, became famous at Clairvaux as a pastor of souls (*Magnificat Antiphon, Evening Prayer*).

Heavenly Father, Saint Bernard was filled with zeal for your house and was a radiant light in your Church. By his prayers may we be filled with this spirit of zeal and walk always as children of light (*Opening Prayer of the Mass, August 20th*).

Father, may the holy food we have received at this celebration of the feast of Saint Bernard continue your work of salvation in us. By his example give us courage, by his teachings make us wise, so that we too may burn with love for your Word, Jesus Christ" (*Prayer after Communion*).

The Roman Missal prior to 1965 reflected Saint Bernard's great love of Our Lady, and his determination to share his devotion to her, by including in the liturgy of his Mass on August 20th a commemoration of the octave of her Assumption, and using the Preface of the Most Blessed Virgin Mary.

Epilogue

Bernard was a valiant defender of the faith, an inspiration to men and women who embrace monastic and religious life, a preacher who converted and reassured innumerable souls, and a peacemaker of extraordinary charisma. Although he loved solitude in which he could commune with his beloved Lord in prayer and meditation, he obeyed God's directions to meet the needs of the Church in the world and, unselfishly, found no contradiction in the spiritual and active qualities of his vocation.

Writing of Bernard in his book '*Saint of the Day*', Father Leonard Foley OFM says,

"To have genuine devotion to God and Mary, and to value the sacredness of life is to prize and treasure one's Christian heritage and beliefs. If we have lost or abandoned some sentimental substance of the Church's inheritance, let us implore Bernard to guide us towards God and our gallant heroes and heroines who lived unselfish and holy lives. Perhaps Christians might seek Mary and the devotional character of their faith. Perhaps novenas, Rosaries, Stations of the Cross, prayers to the Infant Jesus, processions, and lighting candles will become more meaningful and rejuvenating through Bernard's special intercession."

Abbot Dom John Eudes observes that the inspiring writings Bernard based on God's word in Holy Scripture express his own feelings and give to others; "a foretaste of Heaven and the enjoyment of God's inner world. God's word imparts and enables one to relish one's being as no other. God's word, when expressed by holy writers, describes Divine Love with sensitive feeling and motivates one to give oneself to Him more completely. Bernard's words will set the embers of your heart ablaze. His phrases on Divine Love are warm, gentle and exciting. His expressions are sweet, soft and caressing. His writings will give you a pair of wings to soar and experience God."

After the seventeenth century, the Cistercian Order founded by Saints Robert, Alberic and Stephen Harding, and so nurtured by Saint Bernard, divided into the Cistercians of Common Observance (O.Cist) and the Cistercians of Strict Observance (OCSO). The latter are also known as the Trappists after the Abbey of La Trappe in France, one of its eminent Abbots being Armand-Jean de Rance, d.1700. Modelled on Cistercian ideals, it was also strongly imbued with the spirituality of the Desert Fathers, and its penitential life elicited awe and admiration in an age of self-indulgence. In the dawn of the twentieth century, the Church is still blessed with one hundred and sixty houses of monks and nuns of Common Observance and one hundred and sixty-nine houses of

Trappist monks and nuns. Cistercian men and women continue their witness by a life of prayer, study, silence and Christian simplicity, as do thousands of other Benedictines.

Endnote

[1] Bernard's other works include 'On Loving God', 'Eighty-six Sermons for the Whole Year', Meditations on the 'Song of Songs', the 'Book of Precepts and Aspirations' for the guidance of Abbots on Saint Bernedict's Rule; 'On the Duties of Bishops' addressed to Henry, Archbishop of Sens; 'On Consideration', advising the Papacy at the request of Pope Eugenius III; 'On Grace and Free Will' that bases Catholic Doctrine on the principles of Saint Augustine; Homilies on the Gospels ('Missus est'); 'On the Conversion of Clerics', an address to Parisian seminarians; On Psalm 90: 'He who dwells in the shelter of the Most High'; and 530 Letters wherein Bernard meets what he considered his prime responsibility to provide his monks and others with fatherly advice.

Acknowledgements

The CTS gratefully acknowledges recourse to the following sources:

Benedict's Disciples, Ed. D. H. Farmer, Fowler Wright Books, Leominster, 1980.

Christian Monasticism, David Knowles, Widened & Nicholson, London, 1969.

Catholicism, the Story of Catholic Christianity, G. O'Collins SJ & M.Farrugia SJ, Oxford University Press, 2003.

The Papacy, P. Johnson, Weidenfeld & Nicolson, London 1997.

The Divine Office, Collins. London, 1974.

The Penguin Dictionary of Saints, London, 1972.

Butler's Lives of the Saints, Ed. M. Walsh, Burns & Oates, Tunbridge Wells, 1981.

Oxford Dictionary of Saints, D. H. Farmer, OUP, Oxford, 1978.

Encyclopaedia of Catholicism, Harper and Collins, New York, 1995.

History of Christianity, O. Chadwick, Weidenfeld and Nicolson, London, 1995.

The Roman Missal, Burns Oates & Washbourne, London, 1950.

The Daily Missal, Collins, London, 1982.

The Jerusalem Bible, Darton, Longman & Todd, London, 1974.

Book of Christian Quotations, T. Castle, Hodder and Stoughton, London, 1982.

Christian Quotation Collection, H. Ward & J. Wild, Lion Publishing, Oxford, 1997.

Christian Meditation Collection, H. Ward & J. Wild, Lion Publishing, Oxford, 1997.

The Lives of the Fathers, Martyrs, and other Principal Saints, A. Butler, Virtue & Co, London, 1926.

Encyclopedia of Catholicism, Encyclopedia Press, London, 1905.

Libreria Editrice Vaticana, 2009.